CONQUISTADORS

CONQUISTADORS

SUSAN NICHOLS

Britannica
Educational Publishing

Published in 2017 by Britannica Educational Publishing (a trademark of Encyclopædia Britannica, Inc.) in association with The Rosen Publishing Group, Inc. 29 East 21st Street, New York, NY 10010

Distributed exclusively by Rosen Publishing.
To see additional Britannica Educational Publishing titles, go to rosenpublishing.com.

First Edition

Britannica Educational Publishing
J.E. Luebering: Executive Director, Core Editorial
Anthony L. Green: Editor, Compton's by Britannica

Rosen Publishing
Carolyn DeCarlo: Editor
Nelson Sá: Creative Director
Matt Cauli: Designer
Cindy Reiman: Photography Manager
Karen Huang: Photo Researcher

Library of Congress Cataloguing-in-Publication Data

Names: Nichols, Susan, 1975– author.
Title: Conquistadors / Susan Nichols.
Description: First edition. | New York, NY : Britannica Educational Publishing in association with Rosen Educational Services, 2017. | Series: Warriors around the world | Includes bibliographical references and index.
Identifiers: LCCN 2016020885 | ISBN 9781508103783 (library bound) | ISBN 9781508104346 (pbk.) | ISBN 9781508103004 (6-pack)
Subjects: LCSH: America—Discovery and exploration—Spanish—Juvenile literature. | Conquerors—America—History—Juvenile literature. | Conquerors—Spain—History—Juvenile literature.
Classification: LCC E141 .N53 2016 | DDC 970.01/50922—dc23
LC record available at https://lccn.loc.gov/2016020885

Manufactured in China

Photo credits: Cover, p. 3 (conquistador) Eduardo Rivero/Shutterstock.com; cover, p. 3 (background) welburnstuar/Shutterstock.com; p. 7 Library of Congress, Washington, D.C. (LC-DIG-pga-03133)); pp. 8, 18, 22-23 © Photos.com/Thinkstock; p. 9 Encyclopædia Britannica, Inc.; pp. 12-13 © Pixland/Thinkstock; p. 14 University of Texas Libraries; p. 15 DEA Picture Library/De Agostini/Getty Images; pp. 16-17 The Columbian Way Ltda/Moment Open/Getty Images; p. 19 De Agosti/A. Dagli Orti/Getty Images; p. 20 De Agostini/G. Dagli Orti/Getty Images; p. 21 Time Life Pictures/The LIFE Picture Collection/Getty Images; p. 24 (inset) Jon Spaull/Perspectives/Getty Images; p. 26 ©fitopardo.com/Moment/Getty Images; p. 29 Danita Delimont/Gallo Images/Getty Images; p. 31 (inset) Dorling Kindersley/Getty Images; pp. 32-33 © AP Images; p. 35 Archivo Mas, Barcelona; p. 37 PHAS/Universal Images Group/Getty Images; p. 39 Stefano Bianchetti/Corbis Historical/Getty Images; p. 40 ullstein bild/Getty Images; interior pages border and background images © iStockphoto.com/KAdams66 (breastplate cross); © iStockphoto.com/manx in the world (architectural framework), © iStockphoto.com/Luca Corsetti (sabre handle).

CONTENTS

INTRODUCTION

History tells us that in 1492 Christopher Columbus crossed the Atlantic on three sturdy ships—the Niña, the Pinta, and the Santa María—and "discovered" the New World. That world—the North and South American continents—had, of course, already been inhabited by Native Americans for centuries before Columbus's arrival. In addition, Columbus had originally hoped to land in India, on the other side of the world, and was probably frustrated to find the Americas in his way.

Columbus was determined to make sure his discovery was valuable to the monarchs who had sponsored his journey, King Ferdinand and Queen Isabella of Spain. The Spanish sought to establish a powerful empire in the New World, since this land was rich in resources. In this, Columbus was successful; the New World would become a host to some valuable colonies for the Spanish monarchy. However, Columbus's "new world" was already home to many groups of native peoples, referred to as Native Americans. The Spanish had grand plans for these people. They planned to exploit them as laborers to mine the gold and silver they found on their land; they also planned to convert them to Christianity. After all, if the Spanish were about to build an empire, they would want it to be a Christian one.

The Spanish monarchy's desire for a Christian empire was motivated by their own history. In 711, Spain had been conquered by the armies of the Muslim empire. The Muslims, known as the Moors, established a steady government and were

Queen Isabella and King Ferdinand of Spain supported Columbus's journey to India—at least, that is what they thought. He landed on the new continent, claiming it for Spain.

generally tolerant of other religions, but the Spanish fought hard to eject them from their land. As R. Conrad Stein writes in *The Conquistadores: Building a Spanish Empire in the Americas*: "Centuries of conflict with the Moors made Spain a nation of warriors." By 1492, when Columbus sailed, the Muslims had been pushed out of Spain, and Ferdinand and Isabella wanted to make sure Spain became a dominant power once again.

Soon after explorers such as Columbus arrived, another type of man came to the New World: the conquistador, which means "conqueror" in Spanish. These conquistadors were usually skilled, toughened warriors who had fought in the battles against the Muslims and were eager to face new ones in the Americas. Their mission was threefold:

Hernán Cortés, one of the most renowned of the conquistadors, is credited with conquering Mexico for Spain.

to 1) secure new lands for Spain, 2) conquer and convert Native American tribes to Christianity, and 3) obtain as much wealth as possible for the monarchy, which needed it to expand their empire. Many historians agree that the goals of the conquistadors can be summed up as a quest for gold, God, and glory.

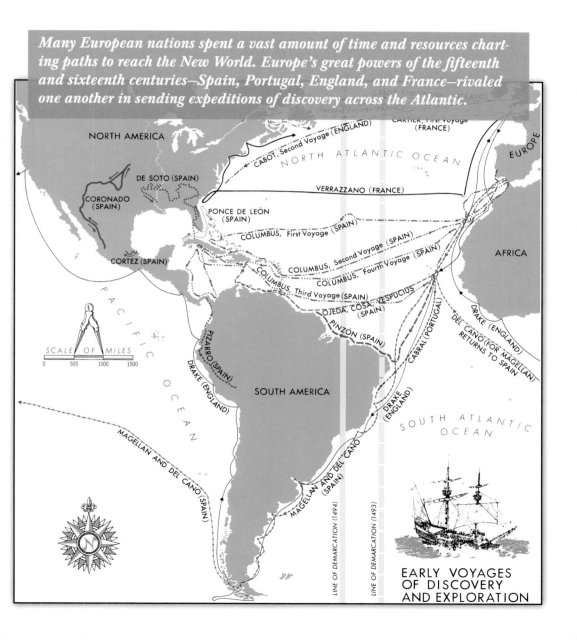

Many European nations spent a vast amount of time and resources charting paths to reach the New World. Europe's great powers of the fifteenth and sixteenth centuries—Spain, Portugal, England, and France—rivaled one another in sending expeditions of discovery across the Atlantic.

EARLY VOYAGES
OF DISCOVERY
AND EXPLORATION

One of the most successful of the conquistadors was Hernán Cortés. He and his men conquered the Aztec empire in Mexico, capturing it and renaming it "New Spain." Other conquistadors, such as Francisco Pizarro and Diego de Almagro, who conquered Peru, also became well-known for their successes across the Atlantic Ocean. But the victories of Cortés and others usually spelled devastation for the Native American tribes they encountered, such as the Aztecs and the Incas. These people were usually enslaved and their way of life destroyed; they looked upon the arrival of the Spanish as a terrible development in their own history.

Unfortunately, the stories of these early conquistadors compelled more Spaniards like them to make the dangerous journey to the New World, seeking glory for Spain and for themselves.

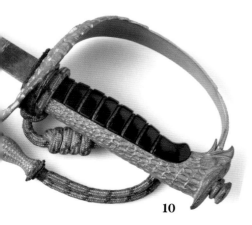

CHAPTER 1
THE QUEST FOR GOLD

History usually celebrates the achievements of the Muslims in southern Europe. In Spain, the Moors built beautiful mosques, baths, centers of learning, and other institutions. They were renowned for producing literature, music, and scientific knowledge. However, despite these achievements, the Spanish aristocracy was eager to defeat the Muslims and erase their influence on their nation. They believed the Moors were pagans, and they wanted to build a Catholic empire to replace their Muslim one.

AN EMPIRE FOR SPAIN

The Reconquista—literally, the "re-conquest"—of Spain took hundreds of years. Finally, in 1492, the last Muslim stronghold in Granada fell to the Spaniards. Spain expelled its Muslim population, though some Moors adopted Christianity and remained.

The Spaniards' next step was to build a new empire, which would take massive amounts of wealth. So, the Spanish monarchs commissioned conquistadors to explore the Americas to find new sources of capital for the new monarchy.

But why would a man want to leave his home in Spain and travel to a new world? One reason was adventure: who knew what this New World had to offer? Another reason was personal prosperity: many young men who did not inherit an income from their families had

The Alhambra, a palace and fortress built by Moorish rulers in the twelfth and thirteenth centuries, overlooks the city of Granada, Spain. The fall of Granada to Christian armies in 1492 marked the end of the Reconquista.

to earn their own living in some other way. Becoming an explorer—with the prospect of striking it rich—was appealing. Many conquistadors were from the lower classes and dreamed of finding a quick way to earn a fortune.

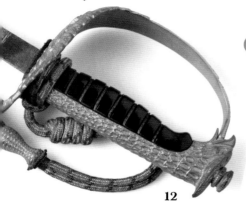

CORTÉS AND THE AZTECS

Hernán Cortés was one of the earliest success stories. Born in 1485 in Medellin, in western Spain, he

left when he was nineteen, seeking adventure and wealth. By 1517, he was living in Cuba, fruitlessly trying to find gold, when a ship captain reported that new civilizations had been discovered in the lands further west. Those lands had gold, silver, and other riches, rumors claimed.

Excited, Cortés set out in 1519 with eleven ships, landing in the port of Vera Cruz, on the coast of what is now called Central America. He and his army of 550 men searched for gold, but found nothing. Cortés communicated with the local people, using gestures and other ways of making them understand what he wanted to find. Eventually, Cortés learned of a land, even further inland, where gold was apparently plentiful. In Vera Cruz, the people referred to that land as "Mexico."

Mexico became Cortés's new goal, despite the fact that it was hundreds of miles away, over rough, mountainous terrain. His men were daunted by the idea of traveling so far into new, unfamiliar territory, which was only accessible by foot. To force them into obeying his orders, Cortés made a bold move: he burned the eleven ships in the harbor of Vera Cruz, giving his men no other choice but to join him.

In 1521, after traveling hundreds of miles, he and his men finally found what they had been looking for—and it certainly must have

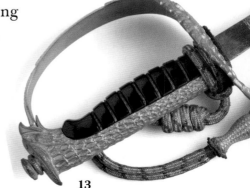

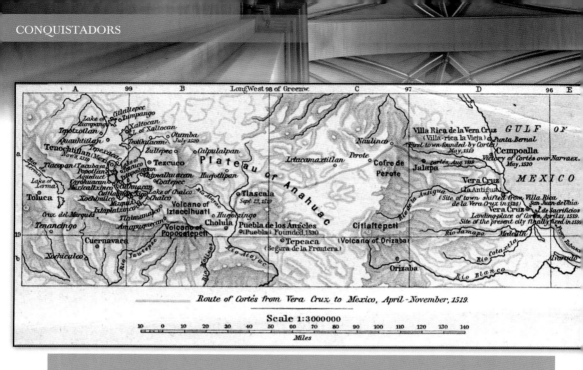

Cortés's journey from Vera Cruz to Mexico is depicted in this map; it is apparent how far inland he and his men had to travel to reach Tenochtitlán.

felt, from their point of view, worth the effort. They discovered the Aztec capital city of Tenochtitlán, a city in which everything seemed made of gold. The Spaniards referred to it as "The City of Dreams."

According to Stein, "The city sat on an island in the middle of a glistening lake. In the center stood pyramids that seemed to pierce the sky. Palaces owned by noblemen radiated out from the center of the city. A system of canals, fed by lake water, brought goods to an enormous city market."

The amount of gold Cortés and his men acquired made them rich beyond their dreams. However, while the Aztec leader Montezuma initially welcomed the foreigners, he soon grew wary of their intentions. In 1520, the Aztecs battled the Spaniards and ejected Cortés and his men from their capital. But Cortés refused to give up his goal now that he knew this land of riches truly existed; with the help of nearby native tribes, who were enemies of the Aztecs, Cortés returned and conquered Tenochtitlán, killing many of its inhabitants and burning much of the city.

In an artist's rendering of central Tenochtitlán, one can see the pyramids and public squares.

THE LEGEND OF EL DORADO

Stories about finding gold in abundance fueled the conquistadors' desire to travel to the New World. One such legend was that of El Dorado, a city of wonder that was rumored to exist in South America.

Sailors and explorers returned from the new lands

with reports of a city that had so much gold, its king powdered his entire body in gold dust daily so that he would resemble a golden statue. The Spanish referred to this king—whom nobody ever actually encountered—as El Dorado, or "the gilded man."

It was also reported that El Dorado and his people celebrated a religious ritual in which they threw gold and jewels in a lake to appease the god who lived beneath its surface. This aspect of the legend made the Spaniards especially eager to find El Dorado, and many explorers set out in search of this lake.

The conquistadors went to great lengths to find El Dorado and its many treasures. When they discovered Lake Guatavita, they completely drained it! They did find some jewels, but they never were able to discover the city of gold.

Lake Guatavita, set in a crater in the Cundinamarca landscape, is a sacred site of the Muisca Indians of Colombia and the origin of the legend of El Dorado.

The Spanish conqueror Hernán Cortés (left) meets the Aztec emperor Montezuma II in 1519.

Cortés called the conquered Aztec kingdom "New Spain." Mexico City, the modern capital of Mexico, is actually built on the ruins of Tenochtitlán.

Other aspiring conquistadors were spurred into action by the success of Cortés, as well as by stories that emerged about possible sites where gold could be found. One such story was that of the Seven Golden Cities of Cibola, which were supposedly constructed of pure gold and were to be found in North America. Antonio de Mendoza, viceroy of New Spain, sent expeditions as far as modern-day Kansas to search for the cities, but they were unsuccessful.

On June 30, 1520—a night known as Noche Triste ("night of sorrows")—Cortés's army retreated from Tenochtitlán, only to return later to conquer the ancient city.

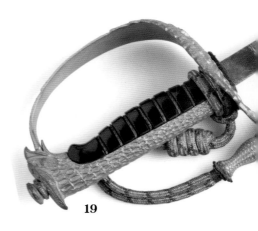

CHAPTER 2

THE QUEST FOR GOD

In 1531, Francisco Pizarro and his companion, Diego de Almagro, traveled on an exploratory mission into the heart of Peru in search of gold. They encountered the Inca people, an ancient civilization of Native Americans.

A priest named Vicente de Valverde was on the expedition with them. The Spaniards, upon encountering the Inca people, were hailed by their leader, Atahuallpa, and several thousand Inca men. Pizarro chose to send Valverde to confront the Incan leader. Addressing

Atahuallpa, Valverde handed him a Bible and informed him that he and his people were now subjects of the Spanish empire.

In response, Atahuallpa threw the Bible on the ground, essentially declaring war on the foreigners. Valverde retreated and reported to Pizarro what had happened, which enraged the conquistador. Pizarro called for a full-scale attack on the Inca

Francisco Pizarro, a famous conquistador, is credited with conquering the Inca and claiming Peru for Spain.

Here, Pizarro is depicted capturing the Incan emperor, Atahuallpa, whom Pizarro executed in 1533.

people, seizing their leader Atahuallpa himself. Pizarro then ordered the shocked Incans to bring him gold or he would kill their king. The terrified Incans obeyed, and Pizarro stunned them by killing Atahuallpa anyway.

CHRISTIANITY IN THE NEW WORLD

This kind of brutality had been practiced by the Spaniards before,

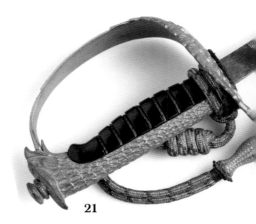

when they were battling the Muslims in Spain. It was also common practice during the time known as the Spanish Inquisition (1478–1834), during which Spanish authorities attempted to eliminate all traces of Islam and Judaism from their land. They did this through torturous methods of investigation, killing and brutalizing people in order to confirm whether or not they were indeed Christians.

The priests who traveled to the Americas with the conquistadors had one mission: to convert the people in this new world from their "pagan" religions to Christianity. They came from

Spanish Jews plead before King Ferdinand and Queen Isabella, while grand inquisitor Tomás de Torquemada argues for their expulsion from Spain, in a painting by Solomon A. Hart.

many different orders, or branches of the Catholic priesthood. Some were Franciscans, some were Dominicans, and many were Jesuits, who were the first religious order to make education of the population part of their holy mission.

According to Thomas, the Jesuits were especially beloved by the Native Americans. This is probably due partly to the fact that the Jesuits made an effort to learn about their lives and even to learn their native languages. The Jesuits also felt a deep sense of pity for the atrocities the Native Americans endured under the Spanish Empire.

FROM CONQUISTADOR TO *ENCOMENDERO*

Once established in the New World, most conquistadors employed an *encomienda* system. The *encomienda*, which means to "entrust", was a grant given by the Spanish monarchy to a conquistador; the grant entrusted the conquistador—now the *encomendero*—with all the land in the area and dominion over its native people.

An *encomendero* commanded the Native Americans living on the land—who were now essentially his slaves—to pay tribute to him regularly. They had to bring him gold or other

23

PEDRO CLAVER, APOSTLE OF THE SLAVES

Pedro Claver was born in Spain in 1581, and he became a Jesuit in 1602. The Jesuits, or the Society of Jesus, had

been established as the empire of Spain spread across the New World. The Church was determined that as more people and civilizations were discovered, they be converted to Catholicism.

In 1616, Claver was sent to work in Cartagena, in Colombia, which was the slave trade capital of the region. Claver was overcome by the terrible plight of the African slaves who were sent to Cartagena; these people were often worked to death, and what lives they were granted were short and filled with suffering.

Claver devoted himself to them, spending 38 years on slave ships and in slave houses, helping to nurse and care for them. He also baptized hundreds of thousands, teaching them his religion. Claver emphasized that people would never convert to Christianity if they were not treated kindly by members of the Christian faith. He said, "We must speak to them with our hands before we speak to them with our lips."

He was canonized by the church in 1888 and is known as San Pedro—or, Saint Peter—Claver, the Apostle of the Slaves.

This photograph captures a contemporary view of the church of San Pedro Claver at sunset in the town of Cartagena, Colombia.

A bird's-eye view of Guanajuato, a beautiful and historic city in Mexico.

forms of payment or else suffer punishment, which could include maiming, beating, or even death. The oppression of the Native Americans was nightmarish. Some depended on their newfound religion, Christianity, for solace and comfort, while others blamed the priests as much as the conquistadors for the miserable state of their lives.

The priests of all the orders built churches throughout the Americas, slowly replacing the local religions. They were successful in some ways, where they were able to blend Christian and native customs. For example, they would merge native festivities with their Christian religious holidays. Another technique was to incorporate native colors into their Christian symbols and church decor.

The local people sometimes rejected this disruption of their lives and their religion. In the 1550s, several Dominican friars had their homes burned to the ground, and thirty Christians were killed in the attack.

CHAPTER 3
CIVILIZATIONS FOREVER ALTERED

T he conquistadors conquered civilizations that were very old, including the Aztec and the Inca. How did they defeat a people on their own terrain so quickly and overwhelmingly?

AN IMPENETRABLE FORCE

The conquistadors were, as mentioned before, hardened warriors. They had spent years in the the Spanish army, battling the Muslim empire and finally ejecting it from Spain. They had learned the strategies of war. They also possessed more powerful weapons than those of the Native Americans. Spanish weapons were made of iron or steel, and their swords, lances, and spears could easily overcome weapons made of wood. The conquistadors' crossbows could send arrows flying much farther than a traditional bow.

Even if the Native Americans could get close to the conquistadors, they couldn't get past one thing: their armor. The Native Americans had never seen a man dressed and plated in metal before, a warrior covered in impenetrable steel.

Then there was one more "weapon" that the Native Americans had never before witnessed: the horse. Horses had not been seen in the Americas until the Spanish conquistadors introduced them. As noted in the PBS documentary *Guns, Germs, and Steel*, "The psycho-

These original swords, used by conquistadors, can be seen at the De Soto National Memorial, in Bradenton, Florida.

logical impact of mounted troops was tremendous." The sound of horses' pounding hoofbeats terrified the Native Americans.

Introducing new weapons, a new fighting style, and new animals to the New World were only some of the ways that the conquistadors would change the lives of the Native Americans forever. Many Native Americans found themselves living in slavery, due to the *encomienda* system. Many had a new religion imposed on them; they were either forced

29

or bribed to convert from the religion they'd practiced all their lives, or they converted because they thought it would bring them advantages—and help them to survive—to practice the same faith as their new conquerors.

European diseases, such as measles and smallpox, decimated the Native American population, and as the population eventually saw an increase again, it, too, was of a different sort. The races that existed before in the New World included white Europeans, Native Americans, and black Africans. The arrival of the conquistadors was about to change this.

MESTIZOS: THE NEW RACE

Many Spaniards married Native Americans, creating what the Spanish called a "new race" in their children. This intermarriage came about because there were simply not as many Spanish women living in the New World yet. Of course, many Spaniards exploited Native American women by kidnapping them, and children were often the result of these crimes.

When intermarriages did take place, they often held a political function. The Spaniards were forging alliances with Native American tribes, and marriage to a Native American noble woman from that tribe was a way to "prove" that they were dependable. These alliances were crucial when the conquistadors wanted to defeat a particular tribe. For example, Cortés was aided by the Maya, Totonaca, and Tlaxcalteca in conquering the

HORSES IN THE NEW WORLD

The conquistadors were expert horsemen, as horseback riding was considered a valuable skill in Spain. They could maneuver quite well in the saddle and attack easily, and the speed of a man on horseback was far superior to that of even the swiftest Native Americans on foot. They used a style of horseback riding called *jineta*, a cavalry style that required speed and skill in the saddle.

They also understood how overwhelming it could be for a Native American to see a man on horseback, controlling a huge animal from the saddle. The powerful image it delivered was intentional: if a man could control such an animal, or if such a beast obeyed the commands of this man, then the man himself was to be feared.

There is a famous story of Hernando de Soto, who was with Pizarro in the conquest of the Incas. De Soto allegedly rode his horse right into the throne room of the Incan emperor; one account states that "the captain advanced so close that the horse's nostrils stirred the fringe on the Inca's forehead."

In this illustration, a conquistador on horseback is escorted by a foot soldier.

Aztecs, and Pizarro was helped in his conquest of the Inca people by the Canari. Garcilaso de la Vega, a writer who recorded the invasion of the Inca people by Hernando de Soto, was himself the son of a Spaniard and an Incan woman.

This new race of people was referred to as *mestizos*, or "mixed." They were of mixed races: the European and the Native American.

In Mexico City, a man performs an indigenous dance as part of the Día de la Raza festivities.

With intermarriages increasing, a new social hierarchy, or *castas*, developed in the new world, and it was based on a person's race.

The highest levels of society were occupied by white Europeans, and the lowest by those of African ancestry. The mestizos were ranked lower than the whites, but could often enjoy privileges that were kept from people of pure Native American ancestry, pure African ancestry, or mixed Native American and African ancestry.

Those at the top of the system were usually landowners and members of the nobility, while those at the lower end of the system were poor, relegated to slavery and servitude in the *encomienda* system.

Racism in the *castas* caused deep resentment among the people of the New World, changing the structure of their society forever.

The new race that the conquistadors brought into being is still evident today in countries that were formerly colonized by Spain. Today in Mexico, for example, 90 percent of the population is *mestizo*. Mexicans celebrate this fact annually on October 12, Día de la Raza—"Day of the Race."

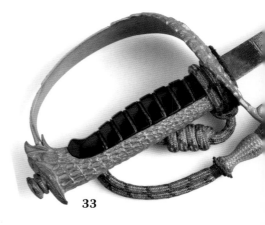

33

CHAPTER 4
FALLING SHORT OF GLORY

T he conquistadors sought gold, God, and glory. They certainly found gold, although not as much as they hoped,
and they succeeded in winning new converts to Christianity, although many Native Americans converted against their
desires. But did they achieve the third goal, glory?

This is a troubling question. If glory means "fame," then many
conquistadors certainly became famous. In addition to Cortés
and Pizarro, there was Pedro de Valdivia. In 1540 de Valdivia
set out with 150 Spaniards and some Native American allies to
explore new territory. He discovered—and conquered—Chile. He
founded the cities of Santiago and Concepción, claiming vast
territories for Spain.

STORIES OF BETRAYAL

However, many conquistadors became known for their cruelty
and brutal methods of conquest, which eventually led to infighting
among the Spaniards themselves. Francisco Pizarro, for example, had a terrible reputation for being vicious with his own men.
His conquest of Peru had been accomplished with the help of his
partner on the expedition, Diego de Almagro. After defeating
the Incan people and seizing their wealth, Pizarro became greedy

Pedro de Valdivia conquered Chile for Spain and founded the cities of Santiago and Concepción.

GOVERNADOR PEDRO DE VALDIVIA

and tried to undermine de Almagro, with the help of newer allies such as Pedro de Valdivia. Eventually, de Almagro was killed by Pizarro's brother, Hernando. In turn, de Almagro's son and a band of his supporters sought revenge; on June 26, 1541, they attacked Pizarro in his palace in Lima and assassinated him. As he died, it is reported that Pizarro drew a cross in his own blood on the ground and kissed it.

The story of Vasco Núñez de Balboa is also troubling. While he was famous for being the first European to see the Pacific Ocean from the shores of the New World, he died quite unfairly. He was known for being kind to the Spaniards who settled in the region he governed, and he enjoyed a good reputation among the people. This popularity caused him to make enemies with other *encomenderos*. Pedro Arias Dávila, a Spanish official, made false accusations against Balboa, and caused others to believe that Balboa had betrayed Spain's government. According to Stein, "In January 1519, Balboa was beheaded in the central square of the Spanish settlement of Acla."

In fact, de Valdivia himself, the conqueror of Chile, also met with a horrible fate. During an attempt to quash a Native American uprising, de Valdivia found himself prisoner of Lautaro, a member of the Mapuche tribe who was leading the revolt against the conquistador. Lautaro demonstrated the same treatment of his prisoner that the Spanish conquistadors had shown to his tribes: he executed de Valdivia.

This painting depicts the death of Francisco Pizarro, who was murdered by men loyal to Diego de Almagro on June 26, 1541.

A LAWLESS NEW WORLD

The most brutal acts of the conquistadors were demonstrated during the *encomienda* system, first implemented by Cortés, who rewarded some of his men with large tracts of land. The death rates among the Native Americans were quite high, and the *encomenderos* did not view the Native Americans as human beings. The devastation caused to the local people's communities and civilization was disastrous. Paul Vickery writes in *Bartolomé de Las Casas: Great Prophet of the Americas* that the *encomienda* system led to a "near extermination" of the Native Americans and that "this system allowed for the exploitation of the weaker by the stronger."

The problem was that the *encomienda* system was not regulated by anyone. The conquistador or the *encomendero* was independent and could do as he pleased. There was no system of law except what the *encomendero* believed and decided. If he were especially brutal, killing or maiming someone for not paying tribute, there was no one to stop him. A Jesuit priest in Peru once wrote that the Spaniards "are very cruel to the Indians, who seem to them to be not men but beasts because they treat them thus to achieve their end, which is silver."

The Spanish Crown was finally convinced that the *encomienda* system was doing significant harm to the local population. They attempted to establish laws that would end the abuse of the native people of the Americas. However, the Laws of Burgos, passed in 1512, and the New Law of the Indies, passed in 1542,

This engraving portrays the conquistador Vasco Núñez de Balboa sighting the Pacific Ocean; in this depiction, he is accompanied by both a priest and a Native American guide.

BARTOLOMÉ DE LAS CASAS

Bartolomé de Las Casas was a Spanish historian and Dominican priest who was born in Seville, Spain, in either 1474 or 1484. He was given an *encomienda* after taking part in the conquest of Cuba. However, while

he worked to convert the Native Americans entrusted to his care as *encomienda,* he understood the terrible ways in which the Spaniards were oppressing the local people.

In 1519, after investigating the abuses of the Native Americans, he convinced King Charles to allow him to establish free cities in the New World; these cities would be inhabited by Spaniards and Native Americans who were not bound to anyone. This new type of living environment, de Las Casas hoped, would spread and be adopted throughout the Americas as an alternative to *encomiendas*; however, the plan failed due to several factors, including resistance by *encomenderos.*

After this failure, de Las Casas chose to become a Dominican priest in 1523 and devoted his life to changing the *encomienda* system. He wrote letters to the Spanish colonial council in which he detailed the abuse he witnessed, and he ordered that Spanish *encomenderos* could not receive the sacrament of confession. His masterpiece is *Historia de las Indias,* which outlines the crimes of Spain against the native population in the Americas.

An illustration of Bartolomé de Las Casas, writing while seated, wearing the robe of a priest and a large crucifix around his neck.

were strongly opposed by the Spaniards living in the New World because they would decrease their control over the people and decrease their profits.

In fact, the system became even worse, and more power would be placed in the hands of the *encomenderos* before it could be taken away. A Dominican priest, Bartolomé de Las Casas, argued before King Charles that the slavery and oppression of the Native Americans was wrong, stating passionately: "All the world is human."

By that point, Spain had begun to replace the conquistadors with governors and administrators in the New World. One of the last conquistadors, Mansio Serra de Leguizamon, who conquered Peru, regretted what the Spaniards had done to the Inca people: "I have to say this now for my conscience: for I am the last to die of the conquistadors."

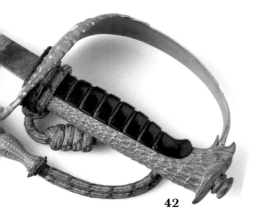

Glossary

castas Castes or class divisions in society.

cavalry Military soldiers who ride on horseback.

commission A task or duty assigned to a person.

conquistador A conqueror.

conversion The process of changing, as in the case of changing one's religion.

crossbow A medieval bow that is anchored on a wooden support and has a device for releasing the arrow.

Dominicans The more common name for the Order of Preachers, a Roman Catholic order of priests.

empire A large number of nations or states brought together under a single authority.

encomendero The grantee, or the individual who has been entrusted with an *encomienda.*

encomienda A system in the early Spanish empire that "entrusted" land and local people to the care of a Spaniard.

Franciscans An order of Roman Catholic priests founded by St. Francis of Assisi.

Jesuits The common name for the Society of Jesus, a Roman Catholic order of priests.

jineta A cavalry style that required speed and skill in the saddle.

lance A long weapon like a spear, used by soldiers on horseback.

mestizo A person of mixed racial ancestry.

oppression Unjust treatment of a person or group of people.

pagan A term used to describe a person whose religion is not considered to fall within the boundaries of one of the world's main religions.

race A division of humankind based on certain outward physical characteristics, not on genetic indicators or any biological concept; a group of people sharing the same general culture, language, and ethnic origins.

tribute Payment made regularly.

viceroy A ruler who governs as a representative of the monarch.

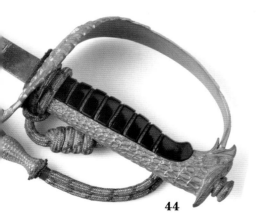

FOR FURTHER READING

Abbott, John S.C. *Hernando Cortés*. San Diego, CA: Didactic Press, 2015.

Baquedano, Elizabeth. *Aztec, Inca, and Maya: DK Eyewitness Books*. New York, NY: DK Publishing, 2011.

Bodden Valerie. *Great Warriors: Conquistadors*. Mankato, MN: Creative Paperbacks, 2014.

Curtis, Matt. *Legends of History: Fun Learning Facts About CONQUISTADORS*. Thought Junction Publishing, 2015.

Gunderson, Jessica. *Conquistadors: Fearsome Fighters*. Mankato, MN: Creative Education, 2012.

Kramme, Michael. *Mayan, Incan, and Aztec Civilizations*. Greensboro, NC: Mark Twain Media, 2012.

Lang, Andrew. *The Conquest of Montezuma's Empire*. San Diego, CA: Didactic Press, 2015.

Matthews, Rupert. *Conquistadors: History's Fearless Fighters*. New York, NY: Gareth Stevens Publishing, 2015.

Ollhoff, Jim. *The Conquistadors: Hispanic American History*. Edina, MN: ABDO & Daughters, 2011.

Stein, R. Conrad. *The Conquistadores: Building a Spanish Empire in the Americas*. Chanhassen, MN: The Child's World Press, 2004.

Vickery, Paul. *Bartolomé de Las Casas: Great Prophet of the Americas*. New York, NY: Paulist Press, 2006.

Young, Jeff C. *Hernando de Soto: Spanish Conquistador in the Americas*. Berkeley Heights, NJ: Enslow Publishers, 2009.

WEBSITES

Because of the changing nature of internet links, Rosen Publishing has developed an online list of websites related to the subject of this book. This site is updated regularly. Please use this link to access this list:

http://www.rosenlinks.com/WAW/conq

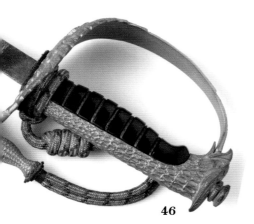

INDEX